T0343105

you are my
sun & my
moon &
all my stars

An Hachette UK Company
www.hachette.co.uk

First published in Great Britain in 2024 by Godsfield,
an imprint of Octopus Publishing Group Ltd
Carmelite House, 50 Victoria Embankment,
London EC4Y 0DZ
www.octopusbooks.co.uk

Distributed in the US by
Hachette Book Group
1290 Avenue of the Americas
4th and 5th Floors
New York, NY 10104

Distributed in Canada by
Canadian Manda Group
664 Annette St.
Toronto, Ontario
Canada M6S 2C8

ISBN 978-1-8418-1570-1

A CIP catalogue record for this book is available from the British Library

Printed and bound in China

10 9 8 7 6 5 4 3 2 1

Publisher: Lucy Pessell
Designer: Isobel Platt
Editor: Feyi Oyesanya
Assistant Editor: Samina Rahman
Senior Production Manager: Peter Hunt

isha tempest

you are my sun & my moon & moon & all my stars

a book to celebrate,
empower and uplift women

GODSFIELD

introduction

What is a woman? She is a nurturing force, a loving partner, a cherished daughter, a supportive sister, and a trusted friend. She embraces countless roles and responsibilities. She creates a warm home, she inspires with her bravery, she leads as a boss, and she contributes as an employee. She is an essential pillar of society, civilization, and the world. However, women often face challenges that undermine their self-worth, self-love, and confidence. They underestimate themselves, despite being more than capable of achieving – and even surpassing – greatness.

Women deserve to be reminded of their inherent strength, and *You are My Sun and My Moon and All My Stars* does just that! This book features timeless poems for women that capture their unwavering determination and fearlessness. It also showcases empowering quotes from inspirational women like Maya Angelou, Toni Morrison, and Frida Kahlo, women who conquered seemingly insurmountable obstacles to achieve phenomenal success. Let their words uplift and empower you as they pay tribute to the indomitable spirit of women who refuse to be held back.

Additionally, this book includes positive and uplifting affirmations that are designed to transform your mindset and foster personal growth. Learning to love oneself is an ongoing journey, and these affirmations serve as a gentle guide, an endless source of inspiration, and a catalyst for empowerment. They possess the ability to motivate you and enable you to overcome negative thoughts, replacing them with positive ones.

So, use these pages to rediscover acceptance for the divine woman that you are. Discover enlightening and simple messages that can counteract toxic thoughts and transform them into positive, uplifting statements. Each empowering declaration will serve as a reminder to release any burdensome energy, allowing you to embrace happiness, authenticity, and presence in every aspect of life. Consider it a gentle encouragement to heal and awaken the goddess within every woman.

Isha Tempest

I alone
hold the
truth of
who I am.

I am allowed
to feel good.

I am
growing
and I am
going
at my
own pace.

Courage
starts with
showing up
and letting
ourselves
be seen.

Brené Brown

Two Women

Ella Wheeler Wilcox

I know two women, and one is chaste
And cold as the snows on a winter waste,
Stainless ever in act and thought
(As a man, born dumb, in speech errs not).
But she has malice toward her kind,
A cruel tongue and a jealous mind.
Void of pity and full of greed,
She judges the world by her narrow creed;
A brewer of quarrels, a breeder of hate,
Yet she holds the key to "Society's" Gate.

The other woman, with heart of flame,
Went mad for a love that marred her name:
And out of the grave of her murdered faith
She rose like a soul that has passed through death.

Her aims are noble, her pity so broad,
It covers the world like the mercy of God.
A soother of discord, a healer of woes,
Peace follows her footsteps wherever she goes.
The worthier life of the two, no doubt,
And yet "Society" locks her out.

I am proof
enough of
who I am
and what
I deserve.

Am I good enough? Yes I am.

Michelle Obama

I am
peaceful
and whole.

I am safe and surrounded by love and support.

Your
perspective
is unique.
It's important
and it counts.

✳

Glenn Close

Nameless Pain

by Elizabeth Drew Barstow Stoddard

I should be happy with my lot:
A wife and mother – is it not
Enough for me to be content?
What other blessing could be sent?

A quiet house, and homely ways,
That make each day like other days;
I only see Time's shadow now
Darken the hair on baby's brow!

No world's work ever comes to me,
No beggar brings his misery;
I have no power, no healing art
With bruised soul or broken heart.

I read the poets of the age,
'Tis lotus-eating in a cage;
I study Art, but Art is dead
To one who clamors to be fed

With milk from Nature's rugged breast,
Who longs for Labor's lusty rest.
O foolish wish! I still should pine
If any other lot were mine.

I am bold,
I am brave,
I am fearless.

I am
my own
reason
to smile.

Nothing can dim the light that shines from within.

Maya Angelou

I am
a strong
woman,
I don't have
an attitude,
I have
standards.

I have
the power
to change.

Welcome, Maids Of Honor

by Louisa May Alcott

Welcome, maids of honor,
    You do bring
In the spring,
And wait upon her.
She has virgins many,
Fresh and fair,
Yet you are
More sweet than any.

I deserve
to be seen.

I am always
capable of
creating
inner peace.

I am no bird;
and no net
ensnares me:
I am a free human
being with an
independent will.

Charlotte Brontë

Wild Nights –
Wild Nights!

by Emily Dickinson

Wild nights – Wild nights!
    Were I with thee
Wild nights should be
Our luxury!

Futile – the winds –
To a Heart in port –
Done with the Compass –
Done with the Chart!

Rowing in Eden –
Ah – the Sea!
Might I but moor – tonight –
In thee!

You can start
late, look
different, be
uncertain and
still succeed.

Misty Copeland

A girl should
be two things:
who and what
she wants.

Coco Chanel

My bravery shines in every act and every decision.

Good riddance
to decisions that
don't support self-
care, self-value,
and self-worth.

Oprah Winfrey

Susan B. Anthony

by Katharine Rolston Fisher

Her life is a luminous banner borne ever ahead of her era, in
lead of the forces of freedom,
Where wrongs for justice call.
High-hearted, far-sighted, she pressed with noble
intrepid impatience,
one race and the half of another
To liberate from thrall.

If now in its freedom her spirit mingle with ours and
find us
toiling at dusk to finish
The task of her long day,
On ground hard held to the last, gaining her goal for
women,
if for her word we hearken,
May we not hear her say:

"Comrades and daughters exultant, let my goal for
you be a mile-
stone. Too late have you won it to linger.
Victory flies ahead.

Though women march millions abreast on a widening
way to freedom,-
trails there are still for women
Fearless to break and tread.

"Keep watch on power as it passes, on liberty's torch
as it
travels, lest woman be left with a symbol,
No flame in her lamp alive.
In the mine, the mill and the mart where is bartered
the bread of
your children, is forged the power you strove for,
For which you still must strive."

Her spirit like southern starlight at once is afar and
around us;
her message an inward singing
Through all our life to run:
"Forward together, my daughters, till born of your
faith with
each other and of brotherhood all the world over,
For all is freedom won."

Embrace
the glorious
mess that
you are.

Elizabeth Gilbert

I attract
love and
abundance.

I am enough.
I have always
been enough.
I will always
be enough.

Your life
is already a
miracle of
chance waiting
for you to
shape its destiny.

Toni Morrison

I'm "wife" – I've finished that

by Emily Dickinson

I'm "wife" – I've finished that –
That other state –
I'm Czar – I'm "Woman" now –
It's safer so –

How odd the Girl's life looks
Behind this soft Eclipse –
I think that Earth feels so
To folks in Heaven – now –

This being comfort – then
That other kind – was pain –
But why compare?
I'm "Wife"! Stop there!

Nothing is impossible. The word itself says I'm possible!

Audrey Hepburn

Self-love is a process and I can choose to enjoy the journey of its discovery.

Aurora Leigh

by Elizabeth Barrett Browning — excerpt

Therefore, this same world
Uncomprehended by you must remain
Uninfluenced by you. Women as you are,
Mere women, personal and passionate,
You give us doting mothers, and chaste wives.
Sublime Madonnas, and enduring saints!
We get no Christ from you, – and verily
We shall not get a poet, in my mind."

The only courage you ever need is the courage to fulfil the dreams of your own life.

Oprah Winfrey

Every day,
I make
choices that
support my
wellbeing and
my self-worth.

Well-behaved women seldom make history.

Eleanor Roosevelt

A wise
girl knows
her limits,
a smart girl
knows she
has none.

Marilyn Monroe

No Coward Soul Is Mine

by Emily Brontë

No coward soul is mine
No trembler in the world's storm-troubled sphere
I see Heaven's glories shine
And Faith shines equal arming me from Fear

O God within my breast
Almighty ever-present Deity
Life, that in me hast rest,
As I Undying Life, have power in Thee

Vain are the thousand creeds
That move men's hearts, unutterably vain,
Worthless as withered weeds
Or idlest froth amid the boundless main

To waken doubt in one
Holding so fast by thy infinity,
So surely anchored on
The steadfast rock of Immortality.

With wide-embracing love
Thy spirit animates eternal years
Pervades and broods above,
Changes, sustains, dissolves, creates and rears

Though earth and moon were gone
And suns and universes ceased to be
And Thou wert left alone
Every Existence would exist in thee

There is not room for Death
Nor atom that his might could render void
Since thou art Being and Breath
And what thou art may never be destroyed.

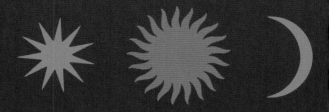

Your crown
has been bought
and paid for.
Put it on your
head and wear it.

Maya Angelou

I have
everything
within me
to reach
the success
I desire.

No Fault in Women

by Robert Herrick

No fault in women, to refuse
The offer which they most would chuse.
No fault: in women, to confess
How tedious they are in their dress;
No fault in women, to lay on
The tincture of vermilion;
And there to give the cheek a dye
Of white, where Nature doth deny.
No fault in women, to make show
Of largeness, when they're nothing so;
When, true it is, the outside swells
With inward buckram, little else.
No fault in women, though they be
But seldom from suspicion free;
No fault in womankind at all,
If they but slip, and never fall.

I gain more
experience
and more
wisdom as
I age.

Take criticism
seriously, but not
personally. If there
is truth or merit
in the criticism,
try to learn from it.
Otherwise, let it roll
right off you.

Hillary Clinton

I can't change
what others
think of me,
but I can
choose how
I respond.

Above all, be the heroine of your life, not the victim.

Nora Ephron

Hope

by Emily Dickinson

Hope is the thing with feathers –
That perches in the soul –
And sings the tune without the words –
And never stops – at all –

And sweetest – in the Gale – is heard –
And sore must be the storm –
That could abash the little Bird
That kept so many warm –

I've heard it in the chillest land –
And on the strangest Sea –
Yet, never, in Extremity,
It asked a crumb – of Me.

I Sing the Body Electric

by Walt Whitman — excerpt

Be not ashamed, women – your privilege
encloses the rest, and is the exit of the rest,
You are the gates of the body, and you are the gates of
the soul.

The female contains all qualities, and tempers them –
she is in her place, and moves with perfect balance;
She is all things duly veil'd – she is both passive
and active,
She is to conceive daughters as well as sons, and sons
as well as daughters.

As I see my soul reflected in Nature,
As I see through a mist, One with inexpressible
completeness and beauty,
See the bent head, and arms folded over the breast –
the female I see.

I breath in healing, I exhale the painful things that burden my heart.

No need
to hurry,
no need to
sparkle, no
need to
be anybody
but yourself.

Virginia Woolf

In every
moment,
I'm exactly
where I
need to be.

On Virtue

by Phillis Wheatley

O Thou bright jewel in my aim I strive
  To comprehend thee. Thine own words declare
Wisdom is higher than a fool can reach.
I cease to wonder, and no more attempt
Thine height t'explore, or fathom thy profound.
But, O my soul, sink not into despair,
Virtue is near thee, and with gentle hand
Would now embrace thee, hovers o'er thine head.
Fain would the heav'n-born soul with her converse,
Then seek, then court her for her promis'd bliss.

Auspicious queen, thine heav'nly pinions spread,
And lead celestial Chastity along;
Lo! now her sacred retinue descends,
Array'd in glory from the orbs above.
Attend me, Virtue, thro' my youthful years!
O leave me not to the false joys of time!

But guide my steps to endless life and bliss.
Greatness, or Goodness, say what I shall call thee,
To give an higher appellation still,
Teach me a better strain, a nobler lay,
O thou, enthron'd with Cherubs in the realms of day!

If you can
dance and be
free and not be
embarrassed,
you can rule
the world.

Amy Poehler

I can create
the life
I've always
dreamed of.

My needs
and wants
are important.

You are never too old to set another goal or to dream a new dream.

Malala Yousafzai

I celebrate
the good
qualities
in others
and myself.

I nourish
myself
with kind
words and
joyful foods.

I found that ultimately if you truly pour your heart into what you believe in - even if it makes you vulnerable - amazing things can and will happen.

Emma Watson

Feeling my
emotions is a
powerful thing.

To My Mother

by Christina Rossetti

To-day's your natal day;
  Sweet flowers I bring:
Mother, accept, I pray
My offering.

And may you happy live,
And long us bless;
Receiving as you give
Great happiness.

I have a
unique and
beautiful
perspective.

It took me quite a long time to develop a voice, and now that I have it, I am not going to be silent.

Madeleine Albright

Advice to the Girls

by Frances Ellen Watkins Harper

Nay, do not blush! I only heard
  You had a mind to marry;
I thought I'd speak a friendly word,
So just one moment tarry.

Wed not a man whose merit lies
In things of outward show,
In raven hair or flashing eyes,
That please your fancy so.

But marry one who's good and kind,
And free from all pretence;
Who, if without a gifted mine,
At least has common sense.

My mother told me to be a lady. And for her, that meant be your own person, be independent.

Ruth Bader Ginsberg

I am still learning so it's ok to make mistakes.

Females

by Charlotte Perkins Gilman

The female fox she is a fox;
    The female whale a whale;
The female eagle holds her place
As representative of race
As truly as the male.

The mother hen doth scratch for her chicks,
And scratch for herself beside;
The mother cow doth nurse her calf,
Yet fares as well as her other half
In the pasture far and wide.

The female bird doth soar in air;
The female fish doth swim;
The fleet-foot mare upon the course
Doth hold her own with the flying horse –
Yea and she beateth him!

One female in the world we find
Telling a different tale.
It is the female of our race,
Who holds a parasitic place
Dependent on the male.

Not so, saith she, ye slander me!
No parasite am I.
I earn my living as a wife;
My children take my very life;
Why should I share in human strife,
To plant and build and buy?

The human race holds highest place
In all the world so wide,
Yet these inferior females wive,
And raise their little ones alive,
And feed themselves beside.

The race is higher than the sex,
Though sex be fair and good;
A Human Creature is your state,
And to be human is more great
Than even womanhood!

The female fox she is a fox;
The female whale a whale;
The female eagle holds her place
As representative of race
As truly as the male.

I am worthy
of investing
in myself.

The way I see
it, if you want
the rainbow,
you gotta put
up with the rain!

Dolly Parton

Past and Future

by Elizabeth Barrett Browning

My future will not copy fair my past
On any leaf but Heaven's. Be fully done,
Supernal Will! I would not fain be one
Who, satisfying thirst and breaking fast
Upon the fulness of the heart, at last
Saith no grace after meat. My wine hath run
Indeed out of my cup, and there is none
To gather up the bread of my repast
Scattered and trampled! Yet I find some good
In earth's green herbs, and streams that bubble up
Clear from the darkling ground, – content until
I sit with angels before better food.
Dear Christ! when thy new vintage fills my cup,
This hand shall shake no more, nor that wine spill.

My weirdness
is wonderful.

I have chosen
to no longer be
apologetic for my
femaleness and
my femininity.
And I want to be
respected in all
of my femaleness
because I
deserve to be.

Chimamanda Ngozi Adichie

There is
room for me
at the table.

When I
forgive myself,
I free myself.

The Crystal Gazer

by Sara Teasdale

I shall gather myself into my self again,
I shall take my scattered selves and make them one.
I shall fuse them into a polished crystal ball
Where I can see the moon and the flashing sun.
I shall sit like a sibyl, hour after hour intent.
Watching the future come and the present go
And the little shifting pictures of people rushing
In tiny self-importance to and fro.

Don't compromise yourself. You are all you've got. There is no yesterday, no tomorrow, it's all the same day.

Janis Joplin

There is a
stubbornness
about me that
can never bear
to be frightened
at the will of
others. My courage
always rises at
every attempt to
intimidate me.

Jane Austen

My body is
beautiful
in this
moment.

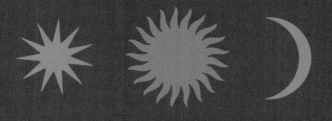

It isn't where you came from. It's where you're going that counts.

Ella Fitzgerald

Women of To-day

by Charlotte Perkins Gilman

Y ou women of today who fear so much
   The women of the future, showing how
The dangers of her course are such and such –
What are you now?

Mothers and Wives and Housekeepers, forsooth!
Great names, you cry, full scope to rule and please,
Room for wise age and energetic youth! –
But are you these?

Housekeepers? Do you then, like those of yore,
Keep house with power and pride, with grace and ease?
No, you keep servants only! What is more –
You don't keep these!

Wives, say you? Wives! Blessed indeed are they
Who hold of love the everlasting keys,
Keeping your husbands' hearts! Alas the day!
You don't keep these!

And mothers? Pitying Heaven! Mark the cry
From cradle death-beds! Mothers on their knees!
Why, half the children born, as children, die!
You don't keep these!

And still the wailing babies come and go,
And homes are waste, and husband's hearts fly far;
There is no hope until you dare to know
The thing you are!

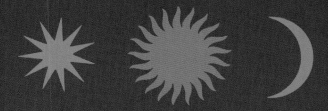

Where there's
hope, there's life.
It fills us with fresh
courage and makes
us strong again.

Anne Frank

I release
what doesn't
serve me.

Nothing is worth more than laughter. It is strength to laugh and to abandon oneself, to be light.

Frida Kahlo

Why We Oppose Pockets for Women

by Alice Duer Miller

1. Because pockets are not a natural right.

2. Because the great majority of women do not want pockets. If they did they would have them.

3. Because whenever women have had pockets they have not used them.

4. Because women are required to carry enough things as it is, without the additional burden of pockets.

5. Because it would make dissension between husband and wife as to whose pockets were to be filled.

6. Because it would destroy man's chivalry toward woman, if he did not have to carry all her things in his pockets.

7. Because men are men, and women are women. We must not fly in the face of nature.

8. Because pockets have been used by men to carry tobacco, pipes, whiskey flasks, chewing gum and compromising letters. We see no reason to suppose that women would use them more wisely.

Every day,
I am
getting better
and better.